ABUNDANTLY
SIMPLE

ABUNDANTLY SIMPLE

EVERYWOMAN'S GRATITUDE JOURNAL

HELEN KAFKA & LAURA HELLEN

INSOMNIAC PRESS

Edited by Mike O'Connor
Copy edited by Lloyd Davis & Liz Thorpe
Illustrations by Laura Hellen
Designed by Mike O'Connor

Canadian Cataloguing in Publication Data

Kafka, Helen, 1959-
  Abundantly simple: everywoman's gratitude journal

ISBN 1-895837-64-2

1. Women - Humor.   2. Canadian wit and humor (English).
I. Hellen, Laura, 1959-   . II. Title.

PS8571.A36A72 1999   C818'.5402   C99-930544-1
PR9199.3.K33A62 1999

Printed and bound in Canada

The publisher gratefully acknowledges the support of the
Canada Arts Council and the Ontario Arts Council.

Insomniac Press
393 Shaw Street, Toronto, Ontario, Canada, M6J 2X4
www.insomniacpress.com

To Gwyneth Paltrow

We would like to thank our families, particularly our parents, Sonia & Michael Kafka and Molly & the late Harry Hellen for their abundant love, patience and material. We also thank Adrienne Ball for opening the door and Mike O'Connor for not slamming it; Ken and Julie for their generosity; Patti and Bluma for their tireless effort; and Laura's daughters, Rachel and Mira Zunder (whom I love and for whom I am truly grateful — L.H.)

INTRODUCTION

While researching our first book, *Cellulite: Fact or Fromage* (unpublished), we came upon a rare, previously undiscovered document. As anthropologists continue to examine the wool content of the parchment (in order to determine eating habits of the Canaanite ewe), it was our Pilates instructor, Norman, who deciphered the hieroglyphics. You can imagine our excitement when we learned that we had unearthed a long-lost scroll from the journal of Lilith—Adam's first wife, who was banished from paradise because she refused to be dominated—truly, the feminist's Holy Grail.

Inspired by the strength of women (literally, from the beginning of time), we turned to women today and asked them, "What are you grateful for?"

With incredible generosity, openness, and unaware of our metal detector, women across the nation let us into their lives, journals and innermost thoughts. Again and again, the diaries we "borrowed" proved to us that we are all one, united in our gratitude. We are all searching for the same things: inner peace, a strong sense of self and a decent manicure.

So now, we welcome you to our journey. We know that once you read the words of these women, you will be able to attain inner peace, wave proudly in sleeveless ... and be grateful.

AUGUST 11th
Chattanooga, Tennessee

I'm grateful that the stray bullet went straight through my living room without disturbing the hutch.

I'm grateful that my motor home is in the better part of town ... today.

I'm grateful that my promotion means I no longer have to wear the paper hat.

I'm grateful for the witness protection program.

I'm grateful that chocolate that has melted can be re-chilled and eaten without losing its flavor.

JANUARY 23rd
Fort Lee, New Jersey

I'm grateful that my second husband Lenny's walker allows him the freedom to vacuum.

I'm grateful that my electrolysist was able to do my entire back in just one appointment.

I'm grateful that my eldest daughter and my ex-husband's new wife, Chloe, share the same homeroom teacher.

I'm grateful for the wisdom that comes with age; it's only in one's 40's that one is able to distinguish anti-depressants solely by size and color.

I'm grateful that my therapist is willing to reduce his fee in exchange for the movie rights to my story.

OCTOBER 14th
Staten Island, New York

I'm grateful that the Chippendale's dancer at my stagette assures me that my Fitz & Floyd pattern is indeed microwave- and dishwasher safe.

I'm grateful that the limo driver was able to use my garter as a fan-belt, keeping us from missing the plane for our honeymoon.

After I tossed the bouquet, I'm grateful that the bridal consultant was able to break up the fist fight between my bridesmaid, Linda and cousin Larry.

I'm grateful that my maid of honor convinced me to go with the headpiece that only holds one beer can. Classy.

I'm grateful that my bridesmaids unanimously decided on the bubble-top and cape combination. It's a flattering silhouette on everyone.

JUNE 23rd
Guntersville, Alabama

I'm grateful that the shipment of Ivana jewelry arrived just in time for the bowling banquet.

I'm grateful for flip-flops—a versatile shoe that's comfortably worn with or without knee-hi's.

I'm grateful that my mother-in-law's electric scooter gives her the freedom to continue her work with Mary Kay Cosmetics.

I'm grateful that the corner 7-Eleven now has shopping carts.

I'm grateful for the silencer on my .45.

DECEMBER 8th
Canyon Ranch, Arizona

I'm grateful that I only passed out twice during aerobics class today.

I'm grateful that the spa liaison assured me that massive hair loss is a natural progression of any weight-reduction program.

I'm grateful for the leaf of romaine and whole grape-fruit for dinner.

I'm grateful that the spa allows me visitation rights with my M&M's.

I'm grateful that the kidney stones I passed helped me reach my target weight.

NOVEMBER 26th
Dubuque, Iowa

I'm grateful that this year's Thanksgiving dinner at Aunt Edna's didn't include a trip to the E.R.

I'm grateful that the firemen were able to coax Uncle Cyril out of the tree without using the tranquilizer dart.

I'm grateful Selma wore her white linen pants so we could screen our holiday slides of the Grand Canyon.

I'm grateful that my mother-in-law doesn't speak English.

I'm grateful for the Right To Privacy Act.

FEBRUARY 18th
Amarillo Correctional Facility, Texas

I'm grateful that my cell mate, Wilma, practices good hygiene.

I'm grateful that the warden gave me permission to display my new line of jewelry on the Home Shopping Network.

I'm grateful that the infirmary scale is off by three pounds.

I'm grateful that the electronic ankle bracelet hasn't stretched my new desert boots.

I'm grateful that the shower stall with the curtain has good pressure.

SEPTEMBER 3rd
Our Lady With Baggage
St. Johnsbury, Vermont

I'm grateful that my tunic allows me to go through many consecutive seasons without waxing.

I'm grateful that the habit keeps my hair-coloring bill to a minimum.

I'm grateful that my wardrobe hides those embarrassing extra winter pounds.

I'm grateful that I'm head-and-shoulders prettier than Sister Wendy— Woof!

I'm grateful that when in Vegas, no one suspects me of counting cards.

MARCH 25th
Fort Lee, New Jersey

I'm grateful that my second husband Lenny's I.V. pole has an additional hook for my fur.

I'm grateful that my second husband Lenny's dialysis machine is grounded and also keeps my coffee hot.

I'm grateful that after the paramedics revived my second husband Lenny, I was fortunate enough to be able to steam out the wrinkles on my linen suit with the defibrillator.

I'm grateful that the magnetic strip on my platinum VISA also activates my second husband Lenny's new pacemaker.

I'm grateful that my second husband Lenny's tremor makes it unnecessary for me to shake his medication.

JANUARY 13th
Clarksdale, Mississippi

I'm grateful that Homer wasn't under the El Dorado when it fell off the cement blocks.

I'm grateful that the excess saliva from Winnifred's constant drooling keeps the bingo dabbers conveniently moist.

I'm grateful that the *Jerry Springer* show allows me to keep up with current family events.

I'm grateful that the pawn shop gave me full retail value for Orville's glass eye.

I'm grateful Lurleen's ability to count to twenty clinched her job as personal trainer to *Hee-Haw* legend Roy Clark.

MAY 20th
Sherman Oaks, California

I'm grateful my new cosmetic surgeon, Julio, has eliminated my need to blink.

I'm grateful that my lip-enhancement surgery was a success. Thanks to the new line of anti-rejection drugs, my body accepted the fat suctioned from my half-sister Edie's thighs.

I'm grateful that my doctor is so compassionate; along with the Prozac, he gave me three repeats on the diuretic.

I'm grateful my six-digit income allows me to be checked in to Cedars-Sinai for "exhaustion" whenever I feel a little over-tired.

I'm grateful that since Charo sprained a hip, my agent says I'm a shoo-in for center square.

JULY 16th
Grand Rapids, Michigan

I'm grateful that menstruation is a good excuse for
_____ (fill in the blank).

I'm grateful that, in a pinch, edible underwear satisfies that emergency premenstrual sugar craving.

I'm grateful that premenstrual water retention allows me to act as a flotation device.

I'm grateful that I only leaked through one layer.

I'm grateful for menstruation—nature's laxative.

APRIL 19th
The Big Top, Missouri State Fairgrounds

I'm grateful that the bearded lady stopped sending me flowers.

I'm grateful that management invested in the new nets.

I'm grateful that the elephant trailer is parked at the other end of the park.

I'm grateful that the seltzer delivery made it just in time for Bobo's matinée performance.

I'm grateful that cotton candy is a low-fat treat.

FEBRUARY 2nd
www.4f4single@wasauwisconsin.com

I'm grateful that the internet allows me to date without getting out of my pyjamas.

I'm grateful that the internet transforms me into a Pamela Anderson look-alike.

I'm grateful that the nude photos of me that ended up on the internet are under a pseudonym.

I'm grateful that my internet date can blab on about himself while I watch the first half of *The Young and the Restless*.

I'm grateful that during cybersex, I can watch the second half of *The Young and the Restless*.

FEBRUARY 29th
Upper East Side, Manhattan, New York

I'm grateful that I was wearing my weekend mink when they splattered me with the red paint.

I'm grateful Sparky's group therapy has addressed his issues of co-dependency.

I'm grateful that the feng shui consultant placed the fountain out of Nana's earshot.

I'm grateful that I found a manicurist who does emergency house calls.

I'm grateful that my cleaning lady rented me her villa at the off-season rate.

MAY 1st
Roosevelt High 25th Reunion
Asheville, North Carolina

I'm grateful for the news that Susie Forrester, home-coming queen for the Class of '74, never *left* home.

I'm grateful that senior cheerleading captain, Mary-Jane Kennedy, now outweighs the team for which she once shook her pompons.

I'm grateful that the members of the '74 boys' championship swim team no longer need to shave their heads to reduce water resistance.

I'm grateful that gravity hasn't affected my double-A bust ... not having been quite so kind to Bambi "The Bombshell" Braithwaite.

I'm grateful that the cafeteria ladies can still carry off wearing a hairnet with panache.

SEPTEMBER 21st
Brooklyn, New York

I'm grateful that when my neighbor's car alarm went off again last night, it really was being stolen this time.

I'm grateful that the artistry of mime is now banned in eleven states.

I'm grateful that my doctor's diagnosis was "E. coli", not "Ebola".

I'm grateful that line-dancing doesn't have its own network.

I'm grateful that elbow grease is just an expression.

MAY 24th
Calabasas, California

I'm grateful that my years of celibacy have given me the freedom to focus my mind on the meditation exercises more easily than the single women.

I'm grateful that my sari has a pocket for my lipstick and gold card.

I'm grateful to the Swami for teaching me that Nirvana has nothing to do with *Courtney* love.

I'm grateful that in the same year I've been able to put away a $2 million nest-egg from my burgeoning small-appliance industry, I have found peace within.

I'm grateful that the Ashram Starbucks has Lactaid.

JUNE 12th
The Love Canal, New York

I'm grateful that not all five toes are necessary.

I'm grateful that my plantar's wart was cured with my fungus medication.

I'm grateful that living years and years here at the Canal has saved me a fortune on waxing.

I'm grateful that the rash didn't flake off in my neighbor's pool.

I'm grateful that the doctor was able to lance the boil that some say had a striking resemblance to Boris Yeltsin.

AUGUST 5th
Fort Lee, New Jersey

I'm grateful that when lightning struck my second husband Lenny's walker, it blackened his chicken just the way he likes it.

I'm grateful that, in the reading of the will, we learned that my second husband Lenny inherited the ark while his sister is saddled with the property in Mesopotamia.

I'm grateful that the gardener was home to change my second husband Lenny's catheter bag so Mr. François could finish my comb-out.

I'm grateful that, now that my second husband Lenny added Viagra to his pill diet, his appetite for chopped liver has returned.

I'm grateful that, during our holiday in Pamplona, my second husband Lenny's new motorized wheelchair allowed him to run with the bulls.

DECEMBER 22nd
Bellevue, New York City, New York

I'm grateful that there really was toast burning.

I'm grateful that the jacket provided by the State not only extends the life of my manicure, but also keeps me from cheating on my diet.

I'm grateful my new medication helps my multiple personalities to agree on where to call for take-out.

I'm grateful that I got my shoelaces back today.

I'm grateful for the book of matches I carry in my purse.

JULY 6th
Milwaukee, Wisconsin

I'm grateful that all twenty-five of us were able to fly stand-by.

I'm grateful that the bus tour of the stars' homes included the birthplace of Arnold Ziffel.

I'm grateful that the package included Mason Reese's marvelous performance in the summer stock production of *A Clockwork Orange—The Musical*.

I'm grateful that the motel dry cleaner was able to locate my good Vulcan ears in time for the Trekkie pot-luck luau and bake sale.

I'm grateful that there was no mosh pit at the Engelbert concert.

NOVEMBER 7th
Ithaca, New York

I'm grateful that the sound of the smoke detector let me know my baked potato was ready.

I'm grateful that my metal allergy doesn't include gold or platinum.

I'm grateful that, now that my husband's job involves traveling forty-nine weeks a year, our marriage is stronger than ever.

I'm grateful that my butcher finally found his severed finger ... in *Mrs. Finkel's* brisket order.

I'm grateful that my gynecologist moved the sock-puppet stirrup covers so the eyes are facing the other way.

JANUARY 31st
Anaheim, California

I'm grateful that Consuela remembered to change the water in the tofu keeper.

I'm grateful to my tarot reader for assuring me that the Hanging Joker is only bad when it's facing east.

I'm grateful that I remembered to remove my bookmark before throwing out this week's *People*.

I'm grateful that, when it caught the sun, the crystal hanging in my lower hallway only burned through one layer of flocking.

I'm grateful that my second fridge easily holds my son's science experiments without crowding Mr. Disney.

AUGUST 18th
Canada (North of USA)

I'm grateful that my new parka emphasizes my waist.

I'm grateful that the igloo has central air.

I'm grateful that the huskies are paper-trained.

I'm grateful for our little summer hideaway in the Arctic.

I'm grateful that Paul Anka didn't write a sequel to "Having My Baby".

AUGUST 27th
Topeka, Kansas

I'm grateful that the plate in my head didn't trigger the metal detector at the airport.

I'm grateful that one of the armrests at the movie theater wasn't moist.

I'm grateful that the guy who threw up on the bus had a *liquid* lunch.

I'm grateful that, while driving, my lazy eye allows me to check my side-view mirror while reapplying lipstick with the rear-view.

I'm grateful that I'm home most of the time so that I won't miss opportunity knocking.

SEPTEMBER 18th
Reno, Nevada

Although I've had a bit of a dry spell, I'm grateful that the Fiorucci sheets on my water-bed are always fresh.

I'm grateful that support hose come in sandalfoot.

I'm grateful that Frederick's carries French maid outfits in "plus" sizes.

I'm grateful that a martini glass can double as a denture soak.

I'm grateful *Cosmo* taught me to always be prepared—I'm never without a corkscrew, a string bikini or Feen-a-Mint.

DECEMBER 11th
Minneapolis-St. Paul, Minnesota

I'm grateful that each time I pronounce "Cuomo" correctly, the producers let me drive the live-eye remote.

I'm grateful for Sports Guy Steve's hot trifecta tip.

I'm grateful that even during the winter months I can maintain my tan with the satellite dish.

I'm grateful that, during rush hour, Chopper Dan can report on a three-car pile-up and an overturned tractor trailer and still get us our bagel order before the coffee is brewed.

I'm grateful for one of the many perks that come with the job: front-row Yanni tickets.

NOVEMBER 20th
Lowell, Massachusetts

I'm grateful that my oven can double as additional storage space.

I'm grateful that the Widow Paterson was found innocent on all charges of solicitation; she's just a friendly neighbor who likes to wear a leather mask—is that such a crime?

I'm grateful that my son's new roommate, Kyle, has such a good sense of color.

I'm grateful that the cyclist I hit was deaf.

I'm grateful for my dashboard compass.

MAY 10th
Berkeley, California

I'm grateful that yoga class has given me a greater awareness of my bikini line.

I'm grateful that the idea of attaining inner peace no longer induces an anxiety attack.

I'm grateful that the dried aromatic grass bundle I added to the fire turned out to be carcinogenic only to mice.

I'm grateful that my Tibetan worry beads were turned in to the information desk at the mud bath pavilion.

I'm grateful that the neighborhood colonic irrigation and hair salon takes coupons.

SEPTEMBER 29th
Scottsdale, Arizona

I'm grateful that when I cough or sneeze, I don't wet my pants.

I'm grateful that Henry's euchre game has improved since the stroke.

I'm grateful for my Clapper.

I'm grateful that my friends still drive at night.

I'm grateful for my Clapper.

SEPTEMBER 7th
Arkadelphia, Arkansas

I'm grateful that my segment on COPS won its time slot.

I'm grateful for the elaborate fireworks display our neighbors purchased at the Dakar duty-free on their last family reunion.

I'm grateful that, when unexpected company drops by, Tang can be mixed with borscht to create a tart summer beverage or a vegetable dip.

After months of worry, I'm grateful that my neighbor Gladys discovered my son's pet boa in her toilet bowl.

I'm grateful that Gladys only required seventeen stitches to mend her little "love bite".

NOVEMBER 1st
Eugene, Oregon

I'm grateful that my facialist says my dehydration can be reversed with a daily regimen of water, masking tape and plenty of embalming fluid.

I'm grateful for the dimmer switch in my bathroom.

I'm grateful for objectivity—knowing nobody can tuck a sweater into a pair of spandex pants.

I'm grateful that, now that I'm going grey, my chin hairs are barely noticeable.

I'm grateful that I decided to take a walk at dusk when the sun could elongate my shadow and help me better accept myself as I am.

JANUARY 17th
Pensacola, Florida

I'm grateful that my treadmill doubles as a clothes-line.

I'm grateful that I could record the entire four-hour miniseries on just one Jane Fonda Work Out tape.

I'm grateful that, even though the camera had no flash, the light from my birthday candles made it possible to capture the moment ... and everyone in the banquet hall.

I'm grateful that shoe-store mirrors are aimed well below the thigh.

I'm grateful that the Pottery Barn has no "you break it, you bought it" policy.

MARCH 10th
Xenia, Ohio

I'm grateful that my new hairdresser graduated at the top of his correspondence-school class.

I'm grateful the dentist was able to save my last remaining tooth.

I'm grateful that there's no expiry date on Jell-O 1-2-3.

I'm grateful that the stamp on the subpoena wasn't canceled and came off in one piece.

I'm grateful that unemployment doesn't interfere with my work.

APRIL 30th
Kemmerer, Wyoming

I'm grateful that, since my last abduction, I'm finally convinced that C2h305 is interested in me as more than just a specimen.

After many hours of experimentation and probing, I'm grateful that the spacecraft dropped me off with cab fare.

I'm grateful that, for the next abduction, they promised they'd cater.

I'm grateful that C2h305 said he would call.

After days of waiting by the transmitter, I'm grateful for the acceptance of the fact the Dr. Gray is right: they _are_ from Mars.

NOVEMBER 28th
P.S. #42, Lackawanna, New York

I'm grateful that there are no parts available for the Ditto machine, so we all get to photocopy!

I'm grateful that, by delegating refereeing duties and a whistle to Gertrude Hierschpiel, I can teach broomball from the heated comfort of the school.

I'm grateful that pre-printed stickers eliminate the need to think up creative words of praise. Well Done!

I'm grateful that April Fool's Day falls on a Saturday this year.

I'm grateful that parent-teacher interviews are monitored on closed-circuit TV.

FEBRUARY 20th
Elwood, Indiana

I'm grateful that the only thing my CAT scan confirmed is that I'm photogenic.

I'm grateful that Froot Loops can be worn as jewelry.

I'm grateful for bomb-sniffing dogs.

I'm grateful that my Aunt Gert's reckless driving supplied me with a muff to match my raccoon coat.

I'm grateful that my new motorcycle helmet doesn't ruin my Friday comb-out.

MARCH 8th
Pittsburgh, Pennsylvania

I'm grateful that my varicose veins divert attention from my cellulite.

I'm grateful that my Thighmaster can double as a mail sorter.

I'm grateful that my electronic make-up mirror supports three settings: Day, Night, and Who-Are-You-Kidding.

I'm grateful that my moisturizer removed the stubborn rust stains from my sink.

I'm grateful that the Epilady adaptor conveniently plugs into the cigarette lighter in my car.

FEBRUARY 27th
Honolulu, Hawaii

I'm grateful that, since the break-up, my sock drawer has never been neater.

I'm grateful that the paper in the *TV Guide* doesn't make my highlighter bleed.

I'm grateful that when the bird droppings landed on my windshield it wasn't in my line of vision.

I'm grateful that my new custom-made jodhpurs make my saddle-bags virtually disappear.

I'm grateful that Momenschantz accepted my application.

FEBRUARY 19th
Wasilla, Alaska

I'm grateful that my recent breakthrough in therapy enables me to exit a room and turn the light off and on only five times.

I'm grateful that my therapist says there will be no surcharge for helping me *own* my anger.

I'm grateful that my multiple personalities allow me a group rate on theater tickets.

I'm grateful that my imaginary friends are tasteful dressers.

I'm grateful for twelve-inch squares of extra-coarse sandpaper.

DECEMBER 15th
Carson City, Nevada

I'm grateful that my Chia Pet doesn't require a leash.

I'm grateful that the market researcher gave me an additional fifty bucks due to the allergic reaction to their new hypo-allergenic moisturizer for sensitive skin.

I'm grateful that, after completing my wine-tasting course, I can now confidently suggest the perfect wine to compliment any TV dinner.

I'm grateful that my La-Z-boy has a cup-holder and a bar fridge.

I'm grateful that I'm the youngest one on the 38-45 demographic chart.

OCTOBER 20th
Dover, Delaware

I'm grateful for the simple beauty of a new pair of black loafers on a crisp fall day.

I'm grateful that I can take comfort in the knowledge that chocolate loves unconditionally.

I'm grateful that television doesn't give off any harmful UV rays.

I'm grateful that the fridge light is sufficient to illuminate the entire kitchen during late-night snacks.

I'm grateful for lazy Sundays and the chance to experiment with make-up.

MAY 31st
Memphis, Tennessee

I'm grateful that the new webbing on the lawn chairs makes them work well with my dining-room table *and* the melamine picnic table out back. At last, year-round comfort without sacrificing beauty.

I'm grateful that, despite her recent amputation, Mom Foster has retained her title as high-scorer on Billy-Rae's mechanical bull.

I'm grateful that the per-family limit on Hamburger Helper was increased to six.

I'm grateful for the news that Aunt Ophelia finally got the recognition she so richly deserved for decorating the rumpus room at Graceland.

I'm grateful that the post office is still using that flattering 1979 photograph.

MARCH 21st
Hartford, Connecticut

I'm grateful that the formula of one part baking soda and three parts vinegar successfully removed the chalk outline from the driveway.

I'm grateful that my ex-husband's Armani suits could be shredded and stuffed into beautiful throw pillows for the barn.

I'm grateful that the picketers weren't within camera view during my "Good Neighbor" segment.

I'm grateful that there was enough fabric to transform the bridal gown from my first wedding into an elegant place setting for twenty-four.

I'm grateful that, in their hasty pre-dawn departure, my household facilitators, Miguel and Francesca, were kind enough to leave behind the antique Aztec hope chest (which makes a perfect boot tray for the tool shed).

FEBRUARY 13th
Valdosta, Georgia

I'm grateful that my neighbor Merle's prosthesis has a socket deep enough to hold the bingo chips.

I'm grateful that my oldest son Earle's mouth guard fit my youngest without any adjustments.

I'm grateful that the security camera caught my best side.

I'm grateful that my 8-track tapes weren't destroyed in the fire.

I'm grateful it's Port-o-Let pick-up day.

MARCH 16th
Decatur, Illinois

I'm grateful that the part of the muffin I ate didn't have the hair in it.

I'm grateful that my hearing loss doesn't affect my ability to eavesdrop.

I'm grateful that my neighbor's dog doesn't find my leg attractive anymore.

I'm grateful that my post-divorce décor passes as minimalism.

I'm grateful I remembered to take my ginkgo biloba.

NOVEMBER 5th
Slidell, Louisiana

I'm grateful that my night-vision glasses are prescription.

I'm grateful that my blind date is up for early parole.

I'm grateful that the entire family was reunited when Grand-Mère Violet gave her final performance at Bob's Burlesque and Bar-B-Q.

I'm grateful that we were able to dislodge the lawn dart from cousin Floyd's forehead without waking him.

I'm grateful for the news that my stepdaughter Tiffany is eligible for the State U. cheerleading scholarship.

MARCH 11th
Dyess Air Force Base

I'm grateful that the fatigues come in various shades of green. I'm a winter.

I'm grateful that latrine duty gives me ample time to soak my fine washables.

I'm grateful that the camouflage helmet makes me look taller.

I'm grateful that the hazing only consisted of wearing blue eye shadow and Frye boots in public.

I'm grateful that the toilet seat is always down.

MAY 25th
Calabasas, California

I'm grateful that the notarized reference letter from my sorority reached the Ashram registrar in time to get me in here, enabling me to learn the concepts of tolerance and acceptance.

I'm grateful that not only is my new Sanskrit name spelled phonetically, but my mantra and PIN number are in the same key.

I'm grateful that meditation satisfies my spiritual hunger while the Ashram Dairy Queen satisfies my sweet tooth.

I'm grateful that the Swami Khullhu has taught me the concept of universal oneness, allowing me the freedom to wear Gucci shoes and a Mizrahi blouse with an Armani suit.

I'm grateful that my husband's dhoti/loin cloth and shawl don't interfere with his golf game.

JULY 7th
Bismarck, North Dakota

I'm grateful that my husband's Water Pik is an excellent tool for removing that stubborn build-up of mildew in the shower stall.

I'm grateful for pepper spray—a tool of self-defense and a convenient steak tenderizer.

I'm grateful that, with a little velcro and an elastic band, I can instantly take off ten years (without the scarring).

I'm grateful that a simple laundry marker can effectively transform even the most unsightly pimple into an attractive beauty mark.

I'm grateful that my guests happily ate the Whiskas-on-a-Ritz when I ran out of pâté.

JUNE 29th
Colorado State University, Colorado

I'm grateful for my extensive vocabulary and the art of embellishment when answering essay questions—style wins over substance every time.

I'm grateful that all-nighters come in pairs: coffee one night; kegger the next.

I'm grateful for my favorite web site: www.termpaper.com.

I'm grateful for Cliff's Notes.

I'm grateful for peripheral vision.

AUGUST 23rd
Gulfport, Mississippi

I'm grateful that, after a whirlwind romance that everyone said wouldn't last, Bob's Big Boy and I were able to remain friends. Lesson learned: never date a celebrity.

After a long winter season, I'm grateful that the dressmaker can reinforce the thighs of my snow pants.

I'm grateful that the Mrs. Miller Wardrobe Exhibit passed through my town.

Even though the airplane was in turmoil, I was grateful that my life-jacket complimented my pastel pant suit.

I'm grateful that my new sandals only reveal one toe, saving me a ton of money on nail polish.

OCTOBER 22nd
Ripley, West Virginia

I'm grateful that weeks of morning sickness kept my appetite in check.

I'm grateful that my Lamaze class is next door to The Bulk Barn.

I'm grateful that, during my third trimester, my unusual culinary palate afforded me the opportunity to experiment with textures—discovering the winning combination of sushi with oatmeal.

Now that the swelling seems to be permanent, I'm grateful to have found a shoe that fits and compliments my maternity wardrobe—my husband's 9 1/2 EEE moccasins.

After a long, hot, dry summer, I'm grateful that when my water broke, I was able to rejuvenate the front lawn.

AUGUST 29th
Dundalk, Maryland

I'm grateful that I have a lovely view of the lake (when my boss' door is open).

I'm grateful that, because of the office composter, my cubicle is a good two square feet bigger than the others.

I'm grateful that my game-saver program allows me to balance a spreadsheet and reach Level 5 of Alien Ship Crusade simultaneously.

I'm grateful that I never have to worry about receiving praise; double-jointedness allows me to pat myself on the back.

I'm grateful that, in a pinch, Liquid Paper works well as a whitener for my boss' coffee.

SEPTEMBER 18th
Ringgold, Georgia

I'm grateful that my grandmother finally returned my Spice Girl halter top.

I'm grateful that, while sitting in the front pew, the holy water didn't stain my new raw-silk outfit.

I'm grateful that my husband's new John Deere now makes us a two-car family.

I'm grateful that, even though my mother just turned seventy, she can still mud-wrestle professionally.

I'm grateful that my TV tray has drawers.

JULY 9th
Camp Taka-Amahya, Moosehead Lake, Maine

I'm grateful that, at 4'11", short-sheeting my bed has no effect on my ability to get a good night's sleep.

I'm grateful that I got back every piece of my clothing from the laundry ... and that grey works well with everything.

I'm grateful that Hobby Hubs get me out of the cabin once a week.

I'm grateful that after a week of meat loaf, hamburgers, spaghetti and meatballs, and chili, the kitchen staff has moved on to chicken.

I'm grateful that the Tuck Shop carries Zantac.

DECEMBER 6th
Montpelier, Vermont

I'm grateful that my postgraduate education permits me to articulate, "Would you _prefer_ fries with that?"

I'm grateful for the sound of birds singing on my window-sill at dawn on a Saturday morning ... and the BB gun I got last Christmas.

I'm grateful that the aromatherapy relaxed me, cleared my sinuses and finally awakened the fertile soil of my soul.

I'm grateful for my strong belief in fate and destiny. How incredibly fortunate to be able to obtain my cousin's standing hair appointment with Mr. Stefan and attend her funeral on the same day. How bitter-sweet.

I'm grateful for Spam.

AUGUST 25th
Seattle, Washington

I'm grateful for call display.

I'm grateful for call block.

I'm grateful for call screening.

I'm grateful for call return.

I'm grateful that the peep-hole I installed gives a slenderizing effect.

APRIL 12th
Brigham City, Utah

I'm grateful that the toilet paper I tucked into my pantyhose was three-ply.

I'm grateful that the Menudo reunion tour will be hitting my home town this summer.

I'm grateful my webbed feet didn't disqualify me from the company swim team.

I'm grateful that Stuart, the hospitality host, took the time to greet me personally as I entered Wal-Mart.

I'm grateful that my cat, Fluffy, hasn't become a side dish at the House of Chan.

NOVEMBER 20th
Lowell, Massachusetts

I'm grateful that my oven can double as additional storage space.

I'm grateful that the Widow Paterson was found innocent on all charges of solicitation; she's just a friendly neighbor who likes to wear a leather mask—is that such a crime?

I'm grateful that my son's new roommate, Kyle, has such a good sense of color.

I'm grateful that the cyclist I hit was deaf.

I'm grateful for my dashboard compass.

MAY 10th
Berkeley, California

I'm grateful that yoga class has given me a greater awareness of my bikini line.

I'm grateful that the idea of attaining inner peace no longer induces an anxiety attack.

I'm grateful that the dried aromatic grass bundle I added to the fire turned out to be carcinogenic only to mice.

I'm grateful that my Tibetan worry beads were turned in to the information desk at the mud bath pavilion.

I'm grateful that the neighborhood colonic irrigation and hair salon takes coupons.

SEPTEMBER 29th
Scottsdale, Arizona

I'm grateful that when I cough or sneeze, I don't wet my pants.

I'm grateful that Henry's euchre game has improved since the stroke.

I'm grateful for my Clapper.

I'm grateful that my friends still drive at night.

I'm grateful for my Clapper.

SEPTEMBER 7th
Arkadelphia, Arkansas

I'm grateful that my segment on COPS won its time slot.

I'm grateful for the elaborate fireworks display our neighbors purchased at the Dakar duty-free on their last family reunion.

I'm grateful that, when unexpected company drops by, Tang can be mixed with borscht to create a tart summer beverage or a vegetable dip.

After months of worry, I'm grateful that my neighbor Gladys discovered my son's pet boa in her toilet bowl.

I'm grateful that Gladys only required seventeen stitches to mend her little "love bite".

NOVEMBER 1st
Eugene, Oregon

I'm grateful that my facialist says my dehydration can be reversed with a daily regimen of water, masking tape and plenty of embalming fluid.

I'm grateful for the dimmer switch in my bathroom.

I'm grateful for objectivity—knowing nobody can tuck a sweater into a pair of spandex pants.

I'm grateful that, now that I'm going grey, my chin hairs are barely noticeable.

I'm grateful that I decided to take a walk at dusk when the sun could elongate my shadow and help me better accept myself as I am.

JANUARY 17th
Pensacola, Florida

I'm grateful that my treadmill doubles as a clothes-line.

I'm grateful that I could record the entire four-hour miniseries on just one Jane Fonda Work Out tape.

I'm grateful that, even though the camera had no flash, the light from my birthday candles made it possible to capture the moment ... and everyone in the banquet hall.

I'm grateful that shoe-store mirrors are aimed well below the thigh.

I'm grateful that the Pottery Barn has no "you break it, you bought it" policy.

MARCH 10th
Xenia, Ohio

I'm grateful that my new hairdresser graduated at the top of his correspondence-school class.

I'm grateful the dentist was able to save my last remaining tooth.

I'm grateful that there's no expiry date on Jell-O 1-2-3.

I'm grateful that the stamp on the subpoena wasn't canceled and came off in one piece.

I'm grateful that unemployment doesn't interfere with my work.

APRIL 30th
Kemmerer, Wyoming

I'm grateful that, since my last abduction, I'm finally convinced that C2h305 is interested in me as more than just a specimen.

After many hours of experimentation and probing, I'm grateful that the spacecraft dropped me off with cab fare.

I'm grateful that, for the next abduction, they promised they'd cater.

I'm grateful that C2h305 said he would call.

After days of waiting by the transmitter, I'm grateful for the acceptance of the fact the Dr. Gray is right: they _are_ from Mars.

NOVEMBER 28th
P.S. #42, Lackawanna, New York

I'm grateful that there are no parts available for the Ditto machine, so we all get to photocopy!

I'm grateful that, by delegating refereeing duties and a whistle to Gertrude Hierschpiel, I can teach broomball from the heated comfort of the school.

I'm grateful that pre-printed stickers eliminate the need to think up creative words of praise. Well Done!

I'm grateful that April Fool's Day falls on a Saturday this year.

I'm grateful that parent-teacher interviews are monitored on closed-circuit TV.

FEBRUARY 20th
Elwood, Indiana

I'm grateful that the only thing my CAT scan confirmed is that I'm photogenic.

I'm grateful that Froot Loops can be worn as jewelry.

I'm grateful for bomb-sniffing dogs.

I'm grateful that my Aunt Gert's reckless driving supplied me with a muff to match my raccoon coat.

I'm grateful that my new motorcycle helmet doesn't ruin my Friday comb-out.

MARCH 8th
Pittsburgh, Pennsylvania

I'm grateful that my varicose veins divert attention from my cellulite.

I'm grateful that my Thighmaster can double as a mail sorter.

I'm grateful that my electronic make-up mirror supports three settings: Day, Night, and Who-Are-You-Kidding.

I'm grateful that my moisturizer removed the stubborn rust stains from my sink.

I'm grateful that the Epilady adaptor conveniently plugs into the cigarette lighter in my car.

FEBRUARY 27th
Honolulu, Hawaii

I'm grateful that, since the break-up, my sock drawer has never been neater.

I'm grateful that the paper in the *TV Guide* doesn't make my highlighter bleed.

I'm grateful that when the bird droppings landed on my windshield it wasn't in my line of vision.

I'm grateful that my new custom-made jodhpurs make my saddle-bags virtually disappear.

I'm grateful that Momenschantz accepted my application.

FEBRUARY 19th
Wasilla, Alaska

I'm grateful that my recent breakthrough in therapy enables me to exit a room and turn the light off and on only five times.

I'm grateful that my therapist says there will be no surcharge for helping me *own* my anger.

I'm grateful that my multiple personalities allow me a group rate on theater tickets.

I'm grateful that my imaginary friends are tasteful dressers.

I'm grateful for twelve-inch squares of extra-coarse sandpaper.

DECEMBER 15th
Carson City, Nevada

I'm grateful that my Chia Pet doesn't require a leash.

I'm grateful that the market researcher gave me an additional fifty bucks due to the allergic reaction to their new hypo-allergenic moisturizer for sensitive skin.

I'm grateful that, after completing my wine-tasting course, I can now confidently suggest the perfect wine to compliment any TV dinner.

I'm grateful that my La-Z-boy has a cup-holder and a bar fridge.

I'm grateful that I'm the youngest one on the 38-45 demographic chart.

OCTOBER 20th
Dover, Delaware

I'm grateful for the simple beauty of a new pair of black loafers on a crisp fall day.

I'm grateful that I can take comfort in the knowledge that chocolate loves unconditionally.

I'm grateful that television doesn't give off any harmful UV rays.

I'm grateful that the fridge light is sufficient to illuminate the entire kitchen during late-night snacks.

I'm grateful for lazy Sundays and the chance to experiment with make-up.

MAY 31st
Memphis, Tennessee

I'm grateful that the new webbing on the lawn chairs makes them work well with my dining-room table *and* the melamine picnic table out back. At last, year-round comfort without sacrificing beauty.

I'm grateful that, despite her recent amputation, Mom Foster has retained her title as high-scorer on Billy-Rae's mechanical bull.

I'm grateful that the per-family limit on Hamburger Helper was increased to six.

I'm grateful for the news that Aunt Ophelia finally got the recognition she so richly deserved for decorating the rumpus room at Graceland.

I'm grateful that the post office is still using that flattering 1979 photograph.

NOVEMBER 18th
Hershey, Pennsylvania

I'm grateful for my employee discount.

I'm grateful for Marge's batch of defective three-legged Turtles (and on the very day that I forgot my lunch!).

I'm grateful that my new apron has insulated pockets.

I'm grateful for my comprehensive dental plan.

I'm grateful for Clearasil and ice-cold milk.

JUNE 21st
www.oursimcha@temple.com

I'm grateful that the cyber-camera was mounted, so I didn't have to do up the back of my dress.

I'm grateful that, despite the fact that my mother-in-law turned up in fuchsia, were able to adjust the transmission into an acceptable shade of peach.

I'm grateful that the modem didn't disconnect until after we finished reading our vows.

I'm grateful that the blue screen camouflaged the Travelodge in Queens to look like the Rainbow Room in Manhattan.

I'm grateful that the virtual reality reception ensured that every guest was seated at Table #2.

SEPTEMBER 14th
Cleveland, Ohio

I'm grateful that all the people in my dreams have the exact same sense of humor as I do.

I'm grateful that my antidepressant 'Kiss-Me Pink' lipstick is SPF 15.

I'm grateful that when I call in sick, I don't need a note from home.

I'm grateful that my insomnia gives me the chance to finish reading, do laundry, build a deck, write my manifesto, solve world hunger and complete my thesis all in one night.

I'm grateful that everyone in group noticed how the *procedure* also eliminated my widow's peak.

JANUARY 11th
Lincoln, Nebraska

I'm grateful that the traffic on the way to work was so heavy I was able to do my hair, make-up and a French manicure.

I'm grateful my voice is not as nasal in my head as it is on my voice mail.

I'm grateful that the brown marker in my purse was a perfect match for my panty hose.

I'm grateful I can still afford the service charge at my bank.

I'm grateful to my co-workers for singling me out to perform gross annual sales in interpretive dance at this year's company picnic.

MAY 26th
Calabasas, California

I'm grateful that, when the truck rounded the corner and forced our rickshaw into the ditch, the flower-based stress beverage kept me totally calm.

I'm grateful that my new head beads don't cause inter-ference on my Walkman.

I'm grateful for the knowledge that the words "I" "LOVE" and "YOU" are one reality because I am I and the master within me and you to love me ... or something like that.

I'm grateful that the solar system wind chimes on my neighbor's hut have only one planet since the storm.

Although it violates Ashram By-Law 34, I'm grateful for my strapless long-line Wonder-Shaper in nude.

JUNE 1st
Tulsa, Oklahoma

I'm grateful that the witness box covered my embarrassing panty-line.

I'm grateful my date's curfew was pushed back to 11.

I'm grateful that jury duty helped influence my boyfriend's probation status.

I'm grateful that my lawyer was able to represent me in my case before being incarcerated for fraud.

I'm grateful for the plea of temporary insanity.

APRIL 1st
North Platte, Nebraska

I'm grateful that color-blindness is accepted when applying for a handicapped parking permit.

I'm grateful that Final Net works as temporary nail glue.

Now that the '70s style is all the rage, I'm grateful that I don't have to replace the shag carpeting and matching drapery in the van.

I'm grateful they can't dust Kleenex for fingerprints.

I'm grateful that, during the impeachment hearings, my favorite network still ran current episodes of *The Guiding Light*.

JULY 29th
Central Falls, Rhode Island

Despite the fact that Miss Cliffcrest Refineries and I had our differences, I'm grateful that I was there to recommend the spray-on adhesive to keep her bathing suit from rising. Oops ... was that my Krazy Glue?

I'm grateful that my job at Hooters provided the training for the swimsuit and heels competition.

I'm grateful that none of my spinning plates fell during the talent competition.

I'm grateful that Miss Congeniality was awarded to Miss Reliable Sewing Machines despite the stern impression given by her uni-brow.

Even though the question presented to me was, "What's your favorite color?", I'm grateful that I could incorporate world peace and rocket science into my answer.

OCTOBER 16th
Paducah, Kentucky

I'm grateful that the crank phone-caller's nose whistle made identification a piece of cake.

I'm grateful that my fingerprint dusting kit is hypo-allergenic.

I'm grateful for my official taster.

I'm grateful that my stalker is seeing someone new.

I'm grateful that the Lorena Bobbitt School of Circumcision has a cancellation.

AUGUST 30th
Hailey, Idaho

I'm grateful for the money I saved by making my own pore-cleansing strips out of packing tape and hairspray.

I'm grateful my jacket was long enough to cover the blood stains.

With all the cutbacks, I'm grateful that I have tenure at the Mint Movie Theatre.

I'm grateful for the stability and predictability of marriage; if my husband is wearing pants, it must be Christmas.

I'm grateful that Uncle Eb was only going 30 miles per hour when he hit the plane.

AUGUST 26th
Bartlesville, Oklahoma

I'm grateful that my neighbor's 'outdoor cat' keeps its distance since we decided Rover should be an 'outdoor dog'.

I'm grateful for the dental floss party favors at the corn roast.

I'm grateful that it wasn't a heart attack after all—just a sugar rush from the quarter pound of double chocolate fudge I had for breakfast.

I'm grateful that my corsage was the perfect size to conceal the beer-nut stain from last night's poker game.

I'm grateful that the private investigator threw in the proofs for free.

AUGUST 24th
Ventura County, California

I'm grateful that, since the mudslide, the real estate agent says the property can now be listed as beach-front.

I'm grateful that the aftershocks moved most of the tchatchkes back to their original positions.

Although the flash fires make it hot, I'm grateful that it's a dry heat.

I'm grateful that the smog index is acceptable when you convert it into metric.

I'm grateful to live in California, where the weather is always perfect.

JANUARY 25th
San Antonio, Texas

I'm grateful that my new X-Acto knife easily cuts away my ex-husband without ruining the entire photo.

I'm grateful that my old breast pump can be recycled and used as a lip-enhancement tool.

I'm grateful that I finally found a horoscope that says I'm going to have a good year.

I'm grateful that the sales clerk who called me "Miss" was not on commission.

I'm grateful that, although the bottled sheep's semen wasn't 100 percent Swiss, the insurance company will still cover the courier's loss.

DECEMBER 20th
McFarland, Wisconsin

I'm grateful for the joyful sound of squirrels frolicking in my back yard.

I'm grateful for the smell of cinnamon that wafts out of the corner bakery.

I'm grateful for the color of sunsets and how it makes the light dance on the koi pond.

I'm grateful for the taste of vegetables harvested fresh from my garden.

I'm grateful for the feeling I get from slow-release lithium.

MARCH 28th
Washington, D.C.

Now that baked Alaska is on the menu, I'm grateful that my uniform is flame-retardant.

I'm grateful that the steam table keeps my perm looking fresh.

I'm grateful that my obscene caller upgraded his cell phone from analogue to digital.

After the passing of my beloved pet Princess, I'm grateful that he lives on in our hearts and macramé.

I'm grateful that my inflatable doll came with a patch kit.

ETERNITY
Heaven

I'm grateful my new set of wings are wash 'n' wear.

I'm grateful that the diaphanous gown comes with a lining.

I'm grateful that there's no area code.

I'm grateful the harp comes with a roadie.

I'm grateful that the dollar is taken at par.

OCTOBER 31st
Salem, Massachusetts

I'm grateful that eye of newt is now available at the No-Frills.

I'm grateful that Crate & Barrel finally got the Esmeralda Cauldron Series in Teflon.

I'm grateful that airbags are standard on next year's model of the Hoover SX3.

I'm grateful for Compound W.

I'm grateful that my mentor, Agatha, was able to attend this year's coven cotillion; she makes 400 look so young.

MAY 11th
Yankton, South Dakota

I'm grateful that with just a few hours' review, I can still help my fourth-grader with her math homework.

I'm grateful that the game of Twister we played snapped my neck back into place.

I'm grateful I had the good sense to put all my money into Beanie Babies rather than a college savings plan.

I'm grateful that my kids' inability to tell time makes bedtime "flexible".

I'm grateful that the children took me to such a fancy restaurant for Mother's Day. They even leave the Sweet 'N Low on the table!

APRIL 23rd
Off-Off-Off-Broadway, New York

Even though the gig doesn't pay much, I'm grateful that my agent could negotiate the rest of my salary in dinner vouchers for "The Colonel".

I'm grateful that my Juilliard training comes in handy when tackling the role of world-renowned mascot, Timmy FishStick.

I'm grateful that my agent negotiated top billing at Chuck E. Cheese.

I'm grateful that my part as the Wind at the Stage Left Dinner Theatre doesn't include bussing tables. Excellent!

I'm grateful that my agent booked my first TV spot. I'm just a little nervous (I hear the puppet wants to direct).

IN THE BEGINNING ...
The Garden of Eden

I'm grateful that my prenuptial agreement granted me a lump sum in exchange for being written out of the Bible.

I'm grateful for gut instinct. When Adam brought home thong underwear, I knew he was cheating.

After Adam left, I'm grateful that I was finally able to drop the annoying twenty pounds without the expense of Nutri-System.

Since we both have our highlights done at The Grecian Room, I'm grateful for the knowledge that Eve's not a real blonde. *Quelle surprise!*

Without invoking the Tenants Act, I'm grateful that my pet serpent's resourcefulness (and Golden Delicious) helped me to evict the couple from my backyard.

Dear Reader:

We're grateful to you for buying our book instead of just reading it over a latté at the bookstore.

We're grateful to our fabulous hair, make-up, photography and air-brushing team who helped us achieve the natural look for the cover photo.

We're grateful for our space pens that allow us to autograph books at any altitude.

We're grateful that our copy of *Simple Abundance* effectively stops the kitchen table from wobbling.

We're grateful for our website:
www.insomniacpress.com\abundantlysimple

What are you grateful for? 'Cause, quite frankly, we're running out of ideas. Visit our website and your daily affirmations could win big prizes! Well, okay, maybe just an autographed copy of *Abundantly Simple*. But it'll be worth it.

Let us know what brings you closer to self-fulfillment.

Gratefully yours,

Helen & Laura,
www.insomniacpress.com\abundantlysimple